50 Things to Know

50 THINGS TO KNOW ABOUT GAME DEVELOPMENT

FROM IDEA TO REALITY

George Ion

50 Things to Know About Game Development Copyright © 2019 by CZYK Publishing LLC. All Rights Reserved.

All rights reserved. No part of this book may be reproduced in any form or by any electronic or mechanical means including information storage and retrieval systems, without permission in writing from the author. The only exception is by a reviewer, who may quote short excerpts in a review.

The statements in this book are of the authors and may not be the views of CZYK Publishing or 50 Things to Know.

Cover designed by: Ivana Stamenkovic
Cover Image: https://pixabay.com/photos/computer-computers-1245714/

CZYK Publishing Since 2011.

50 Things to Know
Visit our website at www.50thingstoknow..com

Lock Haven, PA
All rights reserved.
ISBN: 9781798494868

50 Things to Know About Game Development

50 THINGS TO KNOW BOOK SERIES REVIEWS FROM READERS

I recently downloaded a couple of books from this series to read over the weekend thinking I would read just one or two. However, I so loved the books that I read all the six books I had downloaded in one go and ended up downloading a few more today. Written by different authors, the books offer practical advice on how you can perform or achieve certain goals in life, which in this case is how to have a better life.

The information is simple to digest and learn from, and is incredibly useful. There are also resources listed at the end of the book that you can use to get more information.

50 Things To Know To Have A Better Life: Self-Improvement Made Easy! by Dannii Cohen

---

This book is very helpful and provides simple tips on how to improve your everyday life. I found it to be useful in improving my overall attitude.

50 Things to Know For Your Mindfulness & Meditation Journey by Nina Edmondso

---

Quick read with 50 short and easy tips for what to think about before starting to homeschool.

50 Things to Know About Getting Started with Homeschool by Amanda Walton

I really enjoyed the voice of the narrator, she speaks in a soothing tone. The book is a really great reminder of things we might have known we could do during stressful times, but forgot over the years.

- HarmonyHawaii

50 Things to Know to Manage Your Stress: Relieve The Pressure and Return The Joy To Your Life

by Diane Whitbeck

There is so much waste in our society today. Everyone should be forced to read this book. I know I am passing it on to my family.

50 Things to Know to Downsize Your Life: How To Downsize, Organize, And Get Back to Basics

by Lisa Rusczyk Ed. D.

Great book to get you motivated and understand why you may be losing motivation. Great for that person who wants to start getting healthy, or just for you when you need motivation while having an established workout routine.

50 Things To Know To Stick With A Workout: Motivational Tips To Start The New You Today

by Sarah Hughes

BOOK DESCRIPTION

Are you curious about game development and interested in bringing your idea to a finished product?

Are you an indie game developer that wants to find more about how to achieve success with his games?

Are you an expert with successful projects that wants to maybe find out new things that he does not about the game development industry?

If you answered yes to any of these questions then this book is for you. 50 Things To Know About Game Development by George Ion offers a approach to finding if you have interest for game development and if you have, how to get started with it. Or if you are someone who is already a part of this industry, by reading this book you will find insights into coming up with better ideas, better prototyping and better planning. Most books on game development tell you to just get started and try your best until you get something that works and you will achieve success. Although there's nothing wrong with that, there is a better approach to this industry that can greatly benefit you and your games. Based on knowledge from the world's leading experts only 5 to 10 of 100 published games achieve success, or at least get the money that they invested back, so you have to be smart and make games that people will play and more importantly games that you yourself would play.

In these pages you'll discover what is game development, how to get started, how to learn the skills needed to create games, how to come up with ideas for games, how to decide the scale of your projects and many more topics. This book will help you find motivation to stick to your goals, find the fun in making games and to be prepared for bumps that will inevitably come your way, but I will also show you some things that can be done to overcome those obstacles.

By the time you finish this book, you will know how to make amazing games, design wise not how to actually make the game, and share them with the world so you can earn money or to work in the industry for bigger companies on triple A budget games. So grab YOUR copy today. You'll be glad you did.

TABLE OF CONTENTS

50 Things to Know
Book Series
Reviews from Readers
BOOK DESCRIPTION
TABLE OF CONTENTS
DEDICATION
ABOUT THE AUTHOR
INTRODUCTION
The Beginning Of Your Journey In Game Development
1. Getting Started
2. Choosing A Role
Roles
3. Programmer
4. Artist
5. Sound Designer
6. UI/UX Designer
7. Level Designer
8. Game Designer
9. Tester
10. Making the right decision
The Learning Process
11. Resources
12. Online Courses

13. Books
14. Small Steps Or Big Leaps
15. Game Engines

7 Reasons To Use Unity

16. Unity
17. C# Language
18. Great For 2D And 3D
19. Wide Platform Support
20. Real World Use Cases
21. Extensive Online Services
22. Assets Store
23. Future Roadmap
24. Unreal Engine
25. Learning from Mistakes
26. Frustration
27. Game Jams

Catching the Right Fish

28. Coming Up With Ideas
29. Choosing The Scale Of Your Game
30. Mechanics
31. Art
32. How To Send A Message

Game Design Thought Process

Core Game Design Key Elements

33. Core
34. Player Experience

35. Core Mechanics
36. Theme
37. Core Game Loop
38. Choices
39. Teach The Player How To Play
40. Too Much Story

Plan In Detail

41. Big Picture
42. Milestones And Deadlines
43. Details

Feature Areas of The Game

44. The Three Blocks

Start Creating

45. Prototyping
46. Using Play Testing
47. Scrap What Won't Work

Tuning Your Game

48. Experiment
49. Be Extreme Not Subtle
50. Equate Things To A Common Metric

Bonus 1. Let The Player Fail

Moblie

Bonus 2. Mobile Devices And Games
Bonus 3. Replicas
Bonus 4. Making money
Bonus 5. From One To Another

Bonus 6. Go Hyper Casual
Other Helpful Resources
50 Things to Know

DEDICATION

This book is dedicated to my niece, who is very young but I hope she will share the passion for game development.

ABOUT THE AUTHOR

My name is George Ion, an indie game developer who has worked on a few games, some personal with which I achieved success on a reasonable scale. I have worked for other companies that create games, small ones and big ones like Electronic Arts. I have about 3 years of making games in my background and I like to present myself as a young artist who likes to come up with ideas and use the talents that I have to make those ideas a reality. I am always learning something new and pushing my limits on every new project I begin.

I am currently working on mostly mobile games and looking to help other people start taking their first steps on this path, but also to help veterans of this path who find themselves in rough parts of the journey have an easier time, by organizing better and making designs that are flexible and easy to change in case of disaster.

You can find me on Instagram at @monsta_games0

INTRODUCTION

*"The journey of a thousand
miles begins with one step"*

Lao Tzu.

If you are here first of all let me congratulate you, you chose to take time from your busy life to find out something new, to learn how to develop a new skill or to improve one that is already there. You are amazing and you are not reading this book by coincidence. You are here because you have something to give to the world, an idea, a concept, that sits there in the back of your head waiting for you to take action and transform it to a reality.

This book is here to help you. First of all let me begin with what is game development. Since you are reading this you probably already know, but stick with me because more than often we forget what the core of our intentions is and so we never achieve our goals. Game development is the process through which one or more people come up with an idea and by using the magic of modern times, they work on it and create a finished product that will be sold to other people that like it.

And by magic I mean computers and special software and equipment that can be used to create the pieces of the game development puzzle and also to put them together and put the product out into world. Not the magic spells your game will have the player using to defeat that final boss.

But I like to put it this way. To create an analogy between the game developer: indie or with a team or in a big company and the boss monster called game development who always finds new ways to come at you and mess your code or fry your hard drives. You have to be like the main character of a game, even if you are defeated you have to keep re-spawning and get at it again this time with better prepared and with new weapons and experience to defeat the boss.

So this is what this book will do, it will give you a set of spells, to be precise more than 50 tips, that you can use to finally be the one that wins and sees his or her dreams come true.

Ok, but leaving the analogy aside, analogy that I hope got you in a more game development mindset, let me dig right into the tips and start giving you this amazing information. But first remember why you are reading this book and keep it at the forefront of your mind so it will allow your mind to be open to the new ideas presented here, even if they are not so new for you. Think of it this way, it's all about perspective when doing anything so it may seem familiar for the most part, but it still can bring new insights.

This book is for everyone, but it is mainly written for indie game developers, not people that work for larger companies so please excuse the diving into aspects that may not fit your needs.

Please note that this book is a general guide to approach game development, with information about how to get started, how to create game ideas and how to expand those ideas at a notion level. No tutorials or steps on how to do a certain thing described will be provided.

THE BEGINNING OF YOUR JOURNEY IN GAME DEVELOPMENT

1. GETTING STARTED

Game development is a vast industry with many possibilities and ways to be successful, but it all depends on what is your desire. So do you wish to create games on your own? Or with a small team maybe? Maybe you want to be an artist for the next Triple A title of Ubisoft or EA. Whatever you choose you must first get started. What does this mean? It means to start learning the skills needed for what you are trying to achieve and put those skills to work to fulfill your desire. Getting started is the most difficult part even after you published 10 successful games, why is that you may ask? Because you will always find your comfort zone better than getting started. But if you get up and do the work you will soon see that you did the right decision.

2. CHOOSING A ROLE

In order to get started on learning what it takes to develop games you must first choose your role. The role you have in developing a game is basically what you actually do as a part of creating that game. If you choose to go solo for the indie experience you will have to do everything from art, to programing to design to testing. If you choose to have a small team you might choose the role of the programmer, or the artist, sound designer, we will cover the main roles in a few moments. If you choose to be a graphic designer, programmer, animator, tester, concept artist, any type of role you want, for a big company you will most probably do only the thing you chose to do and also got the job for.

ROLES

3. PROGRAMMER

The programmer is the person who uses a language to talk to the computer, we call that a programming language, and give it specific instructions through which the computer makes the game work, for example a programmer creates the back side of things like health bars, inventory systems, AI behaviors. Every feature in a game works the way it does because it has some instructions linked to it, that were written by the programmer. If you choose this role you have to come up with ingenious ideas to make you code work, to make it cleaner, to make it reusable. Also prepare yourself for being able to fix bugs relaxed and with a smile on your face, because it will be daunting sometimes to handle that.

4. ARTIST

The artist role branches onto many other categories, because there are 2D artists, 3D artists, concept artists, UI/UX artists, animators so there are many possibilities. But there is one main thing that is shared between any of the branches of this tree, the fact that you can draw. In order to create a game that pops out you must know how to draw. The basics of drawing are applicable to any medium. For the indie developer who has to fill this role and knows he lacks the means to create something that will fulfill his vision, the solution would be to pay people to make the art for you, which I recommend the most. If of course the budget allows, otherwise focus on practicing a lot, because the truth is everybody can actually draw, but they lack the practice.

5. SOUND DESIGNER

Being a sound designer is a lot of fun, because you get to create the sounds effects of the game. But also very challenging because everything that will be heard by the player has to be carefully chosen and created so it will provide the best experience that will immerse the player in your game's world. This role is made for those that used to make lots of sound when playing with toys as kids, or still do this in some scenarios as adults, like I do. The thing is that if you want to be a sound designer you must be able to imagine how the game will sound and then reproduce that sound with whatever means you have at your disposal and tweak the raw sounds you create until they are where you need them to be. The indie developer will have loads of fun when coming up with his sounds, but for the soundtrack I strongly recommend paying someone to do it for you, or make it yourself if you have talent in making music too. But here it is a whole other story then drawing, because you really need talent to make great soundtracks, practice will never beat talent when it comes to music.

6. UI/UX DESIGNER

The role of the UI/UX designer is one of a great importance in the game development industry, because the player has to use the user interface to communicate with the game and the game uses it to communicate to the player. It tells the player how many resources or lives he has for example. And the player selects one level or another to play through the use of user interface. Those are just a few examples, more on creating the best UI later. The flow of the game is dictated by the UI and you must choose with great caution the placement of every button and the size of each text element, in order to have a good flow.

7. LEVEL DESIGNER

If you choose the role of the level designer you are in for a lot of fun. Because you get to put together all of the pieces that the artists create and you get to build the environment that the player sees and explores by playing the game. Also you are the one who dictates the main way that player has to follow to finish the game. And also you are the one who can create surprises for the player, to reward him for his explorative nature. This role asks for great imagination and great knowledge of puzzles. Because when you design a level it will be like a puzzle for the player, so the better you are at solving puzzles the better you are at making them, right?

8. GAME DESIGNER

The Game Designer is the one who puts designs the main idea of the game and chooses the best features and mechanics which can really make the game stand out. Also he is the one responsible with balancing the game by making it harder or easier after play testing. This role and the Level Designer are tied together, meaning that they should always be in agreement about a change or a feature, in order to come to the best solution for the game. Later we will cover how to avoid game design mistakes, and how to create better design that will allow you to make better games and faster.

9. TESTER

The tester has one of the most impactful roles in the game development process. Why? Because he is the one that tests the game and gives feedback to all of the other roles about the features and mechanics and also he is the one who finds the bugs that must not be present in the finished and published game. When making you game as an indie developer you will test your game no matter what, but it will be crucial to get other people to test the game too.

10. MAKING THE RIGHT DECISION

In order to choose the role that fits you the best you have to think about what you would like to do the most from the above listed. If you want to have a small team working on a game choose one or more depending on what roles the other people in your team are having. But it is recommended to choose more than one because it can be very useful in the long run. And for the all mighty indie developer, you must fulfill all of the above roles, plus the one of the publisher if you want to go solo about that too.

THE LEARNING PROCESS

11. RESOURCES

When it comes to developing your game you will have to acquire new skills and really grind on those existing ones. So be honest to yourself about what your strengths and weaknesses are and find the right places to dig for information that will give you food for the mind. Which trough practice will make you a pro. If I ask you to think about how many hours did you invested in learning in the past six months, what would your answer be? If the number is bigger than 20 hours let's say you are on the right path. Otherwise think about the fact that in this era internet is traveling at the speed of light and people in this industry use this fact to go today where yesterday was just a fantasy. And they do that by continuously learning and practicing. So get up there and find the resources you need to step up your game, literally.

12. ONLINE COURSES

This is my main recommendation for starting out with game development and for any advanced topic in this field. There are numerous people that worked with the utilities you need to learn for many years and they put together well established courses for you to follow and take your skills to the next level. About any online course site has at least one course that covers the topic you look for. And most of them come with great deals and at very low fees. So get out there and go on a shopping spree of online courses. It will be for your greater good. Most of the websites provide lifetime access to what you buy so you can return any time you want to them, but if you buy it to leave it there it does you no good. Even one video a day will help you a great deal. I am saying this because I myself bought memberships that expired without me even watching 2 hours of the courses.

13. BOOKS

Books are great in my opinion for learning programming languages, they can be consulted any time and provide a lot of resources when you do not understand a concept. Programming languages are sometimes very frustrating to learn and a book is always there for you, waiting to be picked up. Even for software that you may use along your journey a book is a great teacher and always helpful when you do not know that shortcut or how to find that menu that you closed by accident again.

14. SMALL STEPS OR BIG LEAPS

You know yourself better than I do, so take what fits you from this advice: If you are just starting out with anything related to game development, start small and take baby steps. Learn the basics of programming; learn the fundamentals of drawing and art and learn the basics of design. Or if you are experienced or a real pro, take a big leap and learn something that you always avoided learning, maybe some AI behavior or complex procedural level spawning algorithms. Dive right into the resources you just selected for yourself and go through them, as many times needed until you have a stable grip on the notions. Then start to do things on your own, even if it may feel uncomfortable, because it will bring you the greatest outcome when it comes to mastering the skill. We will later cover more about how to come up with ideas and how to design your games in a way that will bring value to the finished product and also make life easier for you.

15. GAME ENGINES

Now in the process of creating a game you will need a game engine. Trust me you need one. If you think about building one you are very brave indeed but you would better invest your time otherwise, because today we have amazing tools available to us, with constant updates and features meant to make game development easier for us. As a tip for the ones who want to build their own, maybe think about getting a job at a company that works on game engines, that would be more fulfilling than wasting months of your life just to make something that kind of works, but not really. So the main game engines I am going to talk about are Unity and Unreal Engine.

Of course there are many other ones out there, but these two are the best in my opinion, with amazing free versions and a lot of helpful assets on their stores. I personally use Unity and next I will give you some reasons why I think it is a great choice for making any type of game you desire. But for Unreal I cannot go in much detail because I have only basic overview knowledge about how it works and how it is used.

7 REASONS TO USE UNITY

16. UNITY

Unity is an amazing engine with very easy to understand interface and tools like prefabs for easier building of your games, animation and physics tools. It is based on scripting, C# and Java-script being the two main languages used. The asset store is a great place to get features that make your life as a developer easier and help you have an overall better experience with the engine. You can of course build all of your mechanics alone, but some of them are very time consuming and hard to accomplish. Things like advanced physics and rigging models.

17. C# LANGUAGE

Unity allows you to use JavaScript and C# as your programming languages. The choice is up to you, because you may come from one specific programming background and be more familiar to one of the two so it will be more natural to use the one you already know something about, right? I personally use C#, which is a great language, at its core it is an object oriented programming language, but in Unity you will use more like a component oriented language, and without going into detail, I highly recommend it because it is very easy to understand, to apply and it is a great tool, that is very looked for even outside the game development industry. There are numerous other places where C# can be used so if you ever get bored of game development you have where to go.

18. GREAT FOR 2D AND 3D

Unity provides to you so many features for both environments that you will be blown away when you take the first look at them. Just to name a few for the RPG creators out there, you have a complete Terrain system which allows you to create huge maps, with tons of details, trees, grass and to paint any kind of texture you like. You can use Shaders to create water, or any other kind of effect you like, you can use NavMesh to let your AI move in the world, and the list goes on and on. I can go into the detail of every aspect of this engine, but that is not the purpose of this book. I am just scratching the surface for you so that after you finish reading you may think: "I am actually interested in investing some time to take a sneak peek into this engine".

19. WIDE PLATFORM SUPPORT

Nowadays cross platform games are a must even for the indie game developer, because think about it, more available platform for your game equals more players. And with Unity you have that at the click of a button. And I am not joking; it supports all major platforms and allows you to create input systems that will work on all of them without you writing thousands of line of code. Just push a few buttons here and there and there you go you have a game working on the web, on standalone, on consoles, on the mobile and so on. In my opinion this is one of the greatest features of this engine.

20. REAL WORLD USE CASES

Unity is not just about games. You can use it to make applications for anything you imagine, from apps that help people navigate a zoo to a sleep tracker app, or whatever you may think of. Also it can be used to create animated films with the bonus of being able to script the behaviors here and there. So overall this engine provides a toolbox for creating what you desire, that rarely lacks what you need.

21. EXTENSIVE ONLINE SERVICES

If you choose to publish an app with Unity, it provides you with the possibility to monetize your app and use analytics to track its evolution. And when

I say app I am referring to the whole variety of platforms we just talked about. Also as a great bonus is that you have constant help from the support teams whenever you have a problem.

22. ASSETS STORE

The assets store is like heaven many times for the indie game developer, because some things are just way to time consuming or out of the scope for some of us and the assets store is there to kindly provide us with whatever we need. It can save you so much time and effort you will never think again about doing some stuff on your own. Of course this comes with the downside that you may feel, like I do sometimes, that you are not staying true to the idea that I make my own assets and I create my game from scratch, but remember that you have a deadline to beat and a certain quality you want to achieve so every hand of help is welcome.

23. FUTURE ROADMAP

The people that created this amazing engine and keep updating it constantly have something called a future roadmap, which is like an in detail story about what they are currently working towards implementing. And that brings value to your games by number one: you know you use a tool that is constantly improved and made better and number two: you know from time what changes may appear and you have the time necessary to adjust your projects so you may not have problems when updating to the new versions.

24. UNREAL ENGINE

Unreal Engine is another great game development engine that is based on visual scripting so this is the one for those of you who have a hard time getting around code and scripting. But hold your horses because when you will open up Unreal Engine for the first time you may have an anxiety attack, because it has so many menus and it is like a maze for a newcomer. But if you stick to figuring out the maze you will be rewarded with straight forward visual scripting tools, beautiful post-processing that for comparison Unity does not have built in. And many other features that can really make you develop the best game possible

25. LEARNING FROM MISTAKES

Always remember that the learning process is continuous and you cannot say "I'm done learning, I know it all", because you may know a lot of things and you may have found success, but you will make mistakes no matter what. It is the human nature, to make some mistakes. This way we come back to what we did and throw a second look and maybe find out that we do not like the way we did that. So the mistake you made helped you in the long run. Mistakes are more than often very hard to deal with in the beginning, but you can learn a lot from them. As an exercise, whenever you make a mistake when developing a game, take a notebook and write it down and also write the solution to it, this will help you train your mind to look out for possible future mistakes and whenever you do it again you have a place to look and solve the issue faster.

26. FRUSTRATION

Most of the times when you learn something new you get frustrated because your results are looking bad, messy, and unappealing. That is perfectly normal, but I know it will still frustrate you a lot, it happens to the best of us. But remember that you are learning and practice makes perfect. And also please use references when starting out, because you learn a great amount from it. But make sure you put your own twist to it. You are just seeking inspiration to nourish your imagination, not copy paste other people's work.

27. GAME JAMS

Game James are contests in which indie game developers and small teams are challenged to create a game in a short amount of time, most of times from 2 days to one week. And this is a great way to perfect your skills, because you will get competitive, also it is great because people will play your game and you will receive feedback, maybe even build a following for later projects. And when making a game in a very short time you will have to stick to what you already know, because trying to find out how to do something when you are pressed by time is not an option. So game jams are a very good opportunity for developers to grow their skills and evolve.

CATCHING THE RIGHT FISH

28. COMING UP WITH IDEAS

Most of the times coming up with ideas for games is the hardest task at hand for a game developer. Because you look around on the market, on any platform and see so much content, so many replicas of the same thing and you ask yourself: Will I ever have an idea that succeeds in this overfilled industry? Trust me, you can. All you have to do is know the secrets of coming up with great ideas for games. And those secrets are: scale, theme, mechanics and art style. If you know how to fill those 4 main components of a game you will come up with amazing ideas.

29. CHOOSING THE SCALE OF YOUR GAME

First and foremost when coming up with ideas for a game, you must decide on the scale of the game. Will it be a small story based point and click side scroller? Maybe you want to make an endless runner for mobile devices. Or you may have a great story to give to the world and you want to create 200 different levels which tell it. The scale of the game is up to you, but it also decides how much time you have to invest in developing the game. Because let's face it more levels and environments equals more art to be done. More NPC's and enemies, means more animations that need to be refined. If the scale grows the time and hard work you have to put in also grows in direct proportion.

30. MECHANICS

The main mechanics of the game are the bread and butter for a successful game. Good controls and amazing new ways for the player to explore the world equals more interest in your game. When coming up with ideas for a game choose a type of game, let's say you want to make a platformer game, then look into the main mechanics of platformer games and remove one, or combine two into one. Mix things up until you find something new and exciting that the people who play your game will find immersive and fun. This removing key features or mixing mechanics up is a great tool that will help you find new ways to give your own twist on the thing that has been done so many times. I will give you more examples so you can really understand the concept: Make a racing game that is based on being last, make a shooter game where you have no bullets, make a survival game with no inventory and so on. By trying out new and what may seem crazy mechanics you will eventually find something that works and build on it. Or store it for a future project if you have no expansion ideas at the moment for it.

31. ART

The style of art you choose is another big factor for two main reasons:

1. More realism asks for more skill and time, but provides the real world feel to your game.

2. Players will not play your game if the art style you chose does not fit what story you want to put out.

The idea is that you have to find a way to convey your story trough the best visual means possible. And most of the times this does not imply a realistic type of art and graphics. You have to link the core of your game (what you want the player to get from playing your game) with the way you display it through the graphics. That is why sometimes a cartonnier look is better, or the retro visual style of pixel art. Speaking of pixel art it is one of my favorite art styles and it is challenging and has so many different ways to express your vision that you will want to use it in all of your games.

32. HOW TO SEND A MESSAGE

Now you have set up your art style, theme, scale and mechanics for your game, well done, but still you must be careful of the way you want to send your message. Or I should say first of all find a message, it has to be less than two sentences long and with a real punch to it. This message is the core of your game. Every mission, task or boss the player has to tackle in the game is there to point to that message. Even hyper-casual mobile games have one, even though it is not as emotional or shaking like other games. The message you choose to send will be picked up subliminally by your players and will make them feel like the game resonates with them.

GAME DESIGN THOUGHT PROCESS

CORE GAME DESIGN KEY ELEMENTS

33. CORE

Your game needs to have a core on which you expand and polish so you get the final build that you are happy with. This core has some key elements that need to be established from the very beginning with great care, because they constitute the "bread and butter of your game". Without them your game will not feel the way it should and most of the times, be unplayable. If the scope of your game is small or medium those core key elements should not be bigger than one sentence, but they have to have a lot of value. If of course you work on a much bigger project the core key features become more elaborate, because the player can interact in much more different ways with the game world.

34. PLAYER EXPERIENCE

Player experience is the first core key feature that you have to choose for your game. As the name of the feature states, it's all about the experience you want the player to have whilst playing your game. This is most of the times comprised of one or two words for smaller scope projects and those words can be along the lines of: frenetic, strategic thinking, creative building, exploring, frustrating or whatever you come up with that fits your idea. I gave those examples so you can make a clear picture in your head about what player experience stands for. You can for sure come up with more direct ideas of a game, but make sure that you break it down and note this key feature, because you need to stick to the core of your game and by establishing this feature you will always know that you want to create this … sort of experience for the player and it will be a lot easier to keep the game on the intended track.

35. CORE MECHANICS

This core feature establishes your core mechanics. Those mechanics are there to give your game life and make it playable and enjoyable. Think about a house, it has core mechanics like doors so you can enter and exit the rooms and a roof to keep the rain out, it also has windows so you can have light during the day. Without those core mechanics a house is inhabitable and it was built for no reason. As the house your game needs those core mechanics so that users can play it. Also the quality of your core mechanics dictate a lot about how much the player will like the game. You can have 20 side mechanics, without your core ones the game is dull and boring.

36. THEME

Your game needs to have a theme, it has to belong in a category, so that you can stick to the most essentials of features and not overcrowd and go over the top with mixing together different themes and fall into the trap of adding more and more stuff in your game that you think is cool, but it does not fit the main theme. By doing that you will just confuse the player and make him quit your game because he does not get the point of all of those extra useless crap you added because you didn't choose a theme at the beginning of your game design. The theme of the game is one of the main keys to unlocking the true potential of a great game, because after all you have to create something that hooks the player and makes him want to explore and play more and more of your game. Also the niche you choose for your game is the factor that tells you how many people would play your game. Go on Steam for example and see what games are best sellers, most of the times those games fall into a niche that a lot of people play. But this does not mean that if a certain type of game has fewer players than others, that type of game should be avoided, not at all. The idea is that by knowing the theme on which you will base your game you will be able to reach your target audience faster and achieve success faster.

37. CORE GAME LOOP

Your game has to have some kind of loop; even if you have levels it can be broken down to a core loop. For example break all of the bricks and collect the keys then move to the next level and do it all over again just in another way, this is a loop. A dungeon based game, it tells the player to kill all of the monsters and collect items then move to the next dungeon, loop starts all over again with other monsters and so on. You have to have got point by now and remember that like all of the other core key features this too must be precisely chosen from the design phase of your game and later on respected.

38. CHOICES

Always keep in mind that you have to give choices to the player. He ultimately is the one who creates the experience he desires through your game, so if he has choices there will be more aspects that will make him feel like he is in control and that he is the one pulling the strings. And that is what you want actually. Because most of the times game developers see through their games and feel like the player should get the whole message as intended. You know your game inside out, but the player does not and most probably never will. For him all that matters is to have fun in your game and feel like he is the one who is taking the decisions no matter what type of game you create. So remember, always give the player at least 2 to 5 choices. You are just the one who creates the fun experience for him, not direct the experience in the way you want with an overly rigid design.

39. TEACH THE PLAYER HOW TO PLAY

Think about your first level of the game and ask how am going to get the player to learn that he has to do this, or that or use that mechanic to be able to finish the level and in turn the whole game. Well you must find a way to teach him. But the way you do that will matter most. Take this for example: I give you my latest game and on the first level I have some text that says "Press SPACE to jump, then arrow keys to move, then slide on that wall" and you try it and you finish the level because I made it simple enough so you can do it. Then you get to the next level and guess what, you already forgot what you need to do.

Because you were not really in the mood for reading all of that and you wanted to play and so on. So you forgot. But what if instead I made the first level so hard that you cannot pass it until you mastered that mechanic and also the way I present it to you is not trough some text on the screen, but with little cues or no cues at all on how to do it. If the player figures it out all by himself, he will keep that in mind for the rest of the game. And then you will have one happy player, satisfied that he himself found the solution for the problem you so kindly created just for this to happen.

40. TOO MUCH STORY

Unless you make a visual novel game focus your attention mostly on the game itself and less on the story. Not that I'm trying to tell that the story is not important but too much focus on story and too much action focused around it makes the developing process harder in the case of things changing or if important 90 degrees turns take place with your game. Focus on the main aspect of your story and on the message it transmits as we already covered. And keep it flexible in case of future changes that may rise. If you want the game you develop to be an amazing experience for the player you must find the complete balance between storytelling and gameplay and also bring value with your story to the game. This may sound a bit hard to achieve, but you sure can do it. Just take notes from other games and try different ways of doing things and remember keep it flexible.

PLAN IN DETAIL

41. BIG PICTURE

At this moment you have your idea and core game design in place and it is time for planning the intricate way to start making it and also to finish it. The first thing is to lay out your vision of the big picture. You most probably played GTA 5, if not I feel bad for you, in that game you did heists and those heists were planned. So remember that board filled with all of the information the guys needed to pull the robbery off. Well you have to do the same thing. In order for you to make a great game you must map out how you want the menu to be, how many levels, how many UI elements, where to put them, how will they look, what kind of sounds you need, when will they play and the list goes on. This idea of mapping out your game will save you loads of time in the making of the game, it will also help you check things off the to-do list and when that will happen you will feel empowered and motivated and in the zone to move forward with the game.

42. MILESTONES AND DEADLINES

The importance of deadlines is crucial in your planning because when they will come closer, the pressure will build and you will start to panic because the game is nowhere near ready because of your lazy days. I'm kidding here but not really. I ask you to take this seriously and set real deadlines, because if they are not real they will not be respected by you or you and your team. So find your real deadline which is let's say one week before the launch date, maybe two, because bugs never cease to come up and slow you down. So being prepared for war is better than not. After you have this date in mind set up milestones between now and the final deadline. How you break it up is up to you. Just after you do, make sure you put those milestones some place where they are visible, preferably most of the time when you work so they keep you motivated and remember to log your work every day. This is will make you feel good when you do more than you expected and it is a good habit actually to log all of your data into datasheets for later research purposes.

43. DETAILS

When it comes to details try to address them too when planning your roadmap for creating your game. But keep a light hand when you sketch them let's say. Because the details change based on how the process of development goes and you will find yourself with plans that have no purpose anymore. And this really is one big challenges of game development, the idea of designing and planning but doing it in a flexible way so if things need to change it will be easy for you. If you can find that balance you will create awesome games I promise you.

FEATURE AREAS OF THE GAME

44. THE THREE BLOCKS

When it comes to develop the game you must have a way of sorting out what you want to implement first and when you want to move on to the next feature and when to add that other secondary thing and when to polish a little. For this you have to keep in mind the three main blocks: Core, Secondary and Polish. Each of those is a part of your finished game and very important in the whole. The question is how to approach implementing those blocks, well first of all you should have a good Core. Implementing the core of your game is probably a half done game, just because your game is playable at this moment. Then add a little polish so you make the game a bit more pleasant, those can be particle effects, screen shakes, sounds. The little polishes will make your game come to life a bit more. After all of that you can start to dig into bringing the secondary features to life whilst of course adding a bit more polish here and there. And finally after most of the features are working and free of bugs, start polishing them to finest detail to give them the final shine you strive for. And lastly create your levels if you go for a level based game. The worst idea ever is to create levels at the beginning or even middle of your project. Just because you will have to go back and change all of things and you will for sure be very frustrated. Trust me a lot of things change when making a game so take my advice for leaving levels last.

START CREATING

45. PROTOTYPING

After you have all of the above listed ingredients at your disposal you have to start the process of combining them. The recipes are up to you, you can look for inspiration in other games for how to use one thing or another, but keep combining until you have what you need. Make as many projects as you like until you have the right prototype that fits your desire of what you want to achieve. And when you find something maybe sleep on it and the next day play test it again so you are sure that you found what you want. Because many times you won't like what you did after some time so it's better to establish the core for good before you move on so you don't have to change entire levels again and again. Trust me I've been there and it is agonizing.

46. USING PLAY TESTING

Play testing is the most important part when you prototype an idea. And by play testing I am not talking about you the developer. You have to let other people play your game as soon as possible to see how they integrate to your game. If you work in a team ask the artist to play the earliest versions of the game so you can change up what is not fitting and keep what is. If you are solo ask a friend. Player feedback is the greatest, because after all, you spend hours upon hours of playing that game and you know how it works, someone new to it may find frustrating things that you do very easy just because you know how the game works and you have more than 50 hours playing it.

47. SCRAP WHAT WON'T WORK

While developing your game, most of the times some features will change because you cannot see into the future and know for sure that all will fall into place like a perfect puzzle. Just keep an open mind to those changes and delete the features that just do not really have a place in your game. Sometimes you may think that a core feature will be just awesome, then make a prototype of the game, work on it a little and after some play testing recognize that it is completely useless and the user rarely has a real use for it. Or it just completely breaks the game and so on. Just scrap it, move on and see how the game works without it. Sometimes it will be perfect, sometimes you will need to come up with another feature that will fill the place of the deleted one. The principle to follow here would be iterate, adapt and let go. As intuitive as this may sound iterate by play testing and receiving feedback from other people, adapt if needed or just let go as said above it won't work in any way.

TUNING YOUR GAME

48. EXPERIMENT

When it comes to tuning your game so it provides the best player experience possible, the first thing you have to do is experiment. Just start playing with values, and take notes about the ones that completely break your game and the ones that have a very small impact. Play around and note every outcome. When you have about a dozen of different combinations go through them again one by one and eliminate those that are useless. But do not be superficial about this, go into every aspect of your game and repeat the process. Also remember that a new set of values for everything in your game can create a whole new experience so that is why experimenting is really important.

49. BE EXTREME NOT SUBTLE

When tuning the values that make your game running you have to remember to be extreme not subtle. What do I mean by that? Well think of it this way, the player has two weapons to buy, one deals 100 damage, and the other 90. That is boring. The player has to feel a difference when for example he upgrades something or when he places another type of tower in a tower defense game, the extreme difference makes the game interesting. And also makes the player feel rewarded with the progress he makes.

50. EQUATE THINGS TO A COMMON METRIC

It can be really helpful to guide yourself when tuning your game by first creating a benchmark system. Choose some values for one thing in your game, for example one monster, and then use this as a guide for the other monsters. And think about you want to achieve with every monster and tune its values according to the benchmark. Also think about establishing standard metrics like number of hits to kill something or time until it reaches the player.

BONUS 1. LET THE PLAYER FAIL

Your game has to have at least one way to be beaten, make sure of that. But you have the let the player fail, because if you create a game that can be finished in one go by every player, you created the most boring game ever. Think about how the player will feel when he cruises to every level of your game. He will feel smart and also not rewarded for learning to use that amazing mechanic you put together with such great effort. Your game will leave a dull feeling to him and make him feel like he wasted his time.

MOBLIE

BONUS 2. MOBILE DEVICES AND GAMES

Nowadays everybody has a mobile phone, and you can see that every time you walk on the street, on the bus, in the train. Everybody has a phone in their hand and looks for ways to kill the time with it when they face boring times like commuting. So you can take advantage of that and start to ship games on this platform too. Even though it may seem an overcrowded market, there is always room for innovation and for you in turn.

BONUS 3. REPLICAS

If you go on Play Store now and search for the most played games you will be surprised to find out that they are the same thing with another name. They are just another redo of the same old match three games or whatever it is. But they have success, because on mobile there are loads of users and they constantly feel the need for another game, even if they find one that they like. So don't be shy of making the same thing with your own twist and getting it on the market.

BONUS 4. MAKING MONEY

When it comes to mobile games there are two ways for making money, maybe three. The first one is selling the app which is something but it may not have loads of success, which is why I said maybe three. The second way is to put the app out for free and monetize it with ads, and after that prompt to the user that he can actually pay so he gets rid of the apps. And last but not least the third is MTX purchases, which to this day are the biggest revenue generators for any company. And I'm not joking, not even triple A games can beat the amount of money people give for another life or that new shiny chest you created. Of course you can monetize with ads and still have MTX purchases, that is up to you.

BONUS 5. FROM ONE TO ANOTHER

If you want to have loads of MTX purchases in your game you have to remember the golden rule of making the user think he is not spending money. Create one type of currency that can be bought with money like coins let's say, and then create another one that can be bought only with coins and is very rare through the game. This way the user thinks he is not actually spending money for the upgraded look of his character, but coins, or diamonds, or smeckels, or whatever you desire.

BONUS 6. GO HYPER CASUAL

The top games right now on Play Store are hyper-casual ones, which involve the same simple process, in an endless manner or in challenging levels. There is no need for story, or loads of graphics, just a well-executed mechanic that is fun to use and feels very addictive to the player. That is actually the main reason for the success of these games, being addictive.

OTHER HELPFUL RESOURCES

Some helpful websites for your game development journey would be:

Udemy - https://www.udemy.com/ (My favorite when it comes to courses)

Itch.io - https://itch.io/ (A very nice portal for you to publish your game and also to participate in jams)

Skillshare - https://www.skillshare.com
(Another online course website that is great for any topic)

READ OTHER 50 THINGS TO KNOW BOOKS

50 Things to Know to Get Things Done Fast: Easy Tips for Success

50 Things to Know About Going Green: Simple Changes to Start Today

50 Things to Know to Live a Happy Life Series

50 Things to Know to Organize Your Life: A Quick Start Guide to Declutter, Organize, and Live Simply

50 Things to Know About Being a Minimalist: Downsize, Organize, and Live Your Life

50 Things to Know About Speed Cleaning: How to Tidy Your Home in Minutes

50 Things to Know About Choosing the Right Path in Life

50 Things to Know to Get Rid of Clutter in Your Life: Evaluate, Purge, and Enjoy Living

50 Things to Know About Journal Writing: Exploring Your Innermost Thoughts & Feelings

50 Things to Know

Website: 50thingstoknow.com

Facebook: facebook.com/50thingstoknow

Pinterest: pinterest.com/lbrennec

YouTube: youtube.com/user/50ThingsToKnow

Twitter: twitter.com/50ttk

Mailing List: Join the 50 Things to Know Mailing List to Learn About New Releases

50 Things to Know

Please leave your honest review of this book on Amazon and Goodreads. We appreciate your positive and constructive feedback. Thank you.

www.ingramcontent.com/pod-product-compliance
Lightning Source LLC
Chambersburg PA
CBHW030954240526
45463CB00016B/2562